Building Success in the Trades
Starting Out & Career Changes

Bill & Georgian Lussier

Purposes of this Handbook
Authors' Notes

This Handbook has Two Purposes:

First, to give an overview of the opportunities and requirements of working in the trades. Over the last few decades, students were largely directed to college, to the exclusion of considering a trade career. Today, tradesmen typically earn between $50,000 – 100,000, and are in high demand.

These jobs cannot be outsourced and offer challenging and meaningful careers. The trades are an essential part of maintaining a healthy and safe society. Anyone who loses power develops an acute appreciation of people who keep the lights on and the water running. Not to mention cell phone access! The authors want to help reverse misconceptions about the dignity of hands-on work.

We offer six examples of successful tradesmen that we know personally. As careers often span forty years, the profiles are divided into early, mid and advanced career stages. We hope these profiles convey a sense of the many options in the trades.

Second, we give advice for those in the mid and advanced career stages. Intellectual, physical and financial factors can cause a professional to make career changes. That may be launching a business, seeking a job as an inspector or trainer, or joining a maintenance department in a municipality. This Handbook includes tips for writing resumes and going to interviews.

Our goal is to provide key learning points that students, parents, educators and experienced tradespeople can build on, through enthusiastic investigation.

Authors' Notes

We use masculine pronouns in this Handbook but firmly believe the trades can be a successful career choice for women. The Resources section includes a You Tube link to an interview Georgian conducted with a woman who owns a contracting business and serves on an Industry Board.

Our experience is within Connecticut: Each state has its own requirements for trade professionals. We provide examples of Connecticut agencies and departments that govern the trades in the Resources section. The reader is encouraged to search for relevant regulatory departments and technical school systems within specific states.

Early Steps

The scariest moment is always just before you start – Stephen King

Working in the trades can lead to life-long success and satisfaction. People with mechanical skills make significant contributions in a wide range of jobs. At different stages in your career you may work on your own, for a small business, for a construction company, or a municipality. Three things make all the difference in your career options:

(1) Solid training and work experience. Think of this as 'paying your dues.'
(2) Acquiring required licenses and taking advantage of learning opportunities.
(3) Self-awareness regarding your work preferences and personal strengths.

Working part-time or summers is an excellent way to test your interest in learning a trade. While your duties may be limited, you can observe master craftsmen and get a sense of typical working conditions. If you are enrolled in a technical school, you are likely to get work experiences, which help you chart a course.

If family members are in the trades, you may think it is the path for you. A word of caution: Becoming a skilled tradesperson requires some inborn talents – not everyone who likes to work with their hands is a natural at reading blueprints and troubleshooting mechanical problems. Get early work experiences and ask for guidance from teachers and parents. Keep an open mind – there is always Plan B.

After 40 years in the field, Bill also emphasizes the importance of reading skills. Everything comes with instructions, and the ability to understand and follow a sequence of steps is essential. Building codes are becoming increasingly complex, requiring solid research and comprehension skills. Whether you work for someone else or want your own business, accurately understanding and fulfilling work orders means you need to make friends with paperwork.

These required comprehension and organizational skills are examples of why becoming a master tradesman is not a fallback option. Rather than saying "college is not for everyone" we need to think in terms of "mechanical jobs are not for everyone". If you are gifted with the natural ability to work with tools and physical systems, don't let anyone steer you in a different direction. Set a goal, be ready to make course corrections, and KEEP GOING!

Work Experience

The only source of knowledge is experience – Albert Einstein

Starting in the Middle Ages, craft guilds defined three skill levels – masters, journeymen and apprentices. The medieval master resembled today's business contractors, who are skilled in their trade, supervise or employ others, purchase materials and sell finished products or services.

Most licensed trades define how much work experience is required to move from an apprentice to a journeyman, to a contractor. Work hours, in conjunction with formal training, are commonly required before a tradesperson can 'sit' for a qualifying exam. In CT, trades boards oversee and update requirements, and are authorized to rule on petitions for special consideration. Many trades require four years of apprenticeship work and over seven hundred hours of classroom training. A vocational high school provides a 'jump' on classroom hours.

A trade such as Glazier may not have well-defined requirements or a governing association, leaving the interested person on his own to seek out work experiences through an apprenticeship.

If your state requires a license (not a registration) to perform trade services, there are likely established rules for enrolling as an apprentice and accumulating work hours. Licenses require taking an exam – registrations generally do not.

Seek control of your work experience – much as you would when declaring a major course of college study. If you are with a union program, your experience may focus on commercial jobs; in a small family business, the work projects may be exclusively residential. As with any profession, getting diverse experiences produces a more well-rounded tradesperson. While conventional wisdom is 'never volunteer', be alert to opportunities that widen your horizons.

 Many trades require formal apprenticeships. A common mistake is to work for a company that does not enroll as a program sponsor. You could lose years of uncredited experience. This is time wasted – move on if your work hours are not counted towards license requirements.

Training & Education

An investment in knowledge pays the best interest – Benjamin Franklin

Becoming a professional tradesperson requires a commitment to learning relevant principles, practices and skills. This learning never stops – the professional stays current with new requirements, products and work methods.

While various trades require specific skills, there are <u>common requirements</u>:

- **Manual dexterity** - the ability to make coordinated hand and finger movements to grasp and manipulate objects.
- **Mechanical aptitude** - the ability to take things apart, put them back together, and fix them.
- **Spatial reasoning**- the ability to think about objects in three dimensions and to draw conclusions about those objects from limited information.
- **Math skills** - the ability to make computations and to use measuring tools and rulers.
- **Reading skills** – the ability to comprehend material and master a technical vocabulary.

In addition to trade-specific coursework, technical high school students and apprentices typically study trade and business math; blueprint reading; building codes; systems installation; science principles and safety requirements and practices. As professionals assume higher levels of responsibilities, they need to sharpen their critical thinking, analytical, quantitative and problem-solving skills

<u>Advanced career jobs</u> typically require additional skills, in areas such as:

- Project management and use of sophisticated technology;
- Supervisory responsibilities and maintaining safety incident logs;
- Gathering data and statistics and writing reports;
- Managing budgets and documenting cost over-runs;
- Experience with solar systems, health facilities and governments.

In addition, <u>business owners</u> need to oversee multiple functions, including:

- Knowledge of labor laws and establishment of employee standards;
- Familiarity with accounting terminology and maintenance of bookkeeping;
- Insurance coverage for tools, trucks, inventory, employees and damages;
- Customer service practices; tracking results and making improvements;
- Compliance with building codes, tax laws, and local ordinances.

How to get the training and information you need:

Trade schools offer a firm career start; you can graduate ahead of the game, having fulfilled the educational requirements of an apprenticeship.

Apprenticeship training through a technical school system or union organization will keep your career moving forward – Bill taught night classes for many years.

Continuing education requirements in states such as Connecticut are mandated for several trades. While it can seem like a nuisance to free up a day for training, it is one good way to stay current with building code changes and state laws.

Community and Vocational colleges offer affordable technical and business training, including machine technology, entrepreneurship and communications.

Industry associations typically offer courses and certificate programs; some are on-line. Trade shows hold seminars, demonstrate new products and give you access to experts and resources.

Civic organizations such as a Chamber of Commerce and Rotary help you connect with professionals who can point out reliable educational sources. Community non-profits may offer career development and guidance, such as "Beat the Street" in Meriden, CT.

Collaboration with accountants, lawyers, and marketing professionals can give you access to business workshops and individual coaching. As a business owner, show your commitment – ask questions.

Self-study can pay big dividends. Develop the discipline to tackle a subject, one chapter at a time. Whether on-line or using a physical book, make notes.

Videos, such as The History Channel's "Modern Marvels" and the PBS "Good Works: Masters of the Building Arts" can increase your knowledge and appreciation of science, craftsmanship and human ingenuity.

Maintain a library. Create an accessible way to locate information you've gained. Building codes, business books, workshop/ course materials, and online tutorials can be housed in a common area for quick reference. Your local library is also a great resource; look for classes and speakers, in addition to reading and multi-media materials.

Everyone has areas where they need some additional support: A tutor can have a life-changing impact on career success. For example, you may be good at some types of math, but not others. A tutor can determine how to work with your thinking style and give you new ways to solve a math problem. Find the help you need -- whether classes, community group mentors or individual tutors.

Licenses, Certifications ... and College?

Licensing requirements vary by state and regional areas. Where required, licenses are intended to lessen health and safety risks to the general public; often they are governed by departments of consumer protection. Licenses also serve tradesmen; by meeting educational and experience standards, and passing a test, a person has established himself as a professional. This helps to reduce liability risks for the tradesperson and the company he works for or owns. Taking continuing education classes also helps the tradesperson comply with laws and regulations, which reduces the risk of performing work that is not up to current standards. A failed inspection requires expensive rework.

For example: The classes Bill teaches to prepare people to sit for a CT Building Code Enforcement exam are eight months long: Students include contractors and inspectors, as well as some architects and engineers. They devote two days of their workweeks in class, in addition to completing homework, studying the complex code requirements for building, mechanical, plumbing and electrical trades. People with even thirty years of experience are surprised at what they do not know – saying "That's not true, is it?"

Licensing can set a firm foundation for the tradesperson, and continual learning expands his knowledge base. The building codes get more complicated each year: Currently, CT uses over 2,000 pages of codes, including the International Residential Code, the International Building Code, the National Electrical Code, the Energy Conservation Code, International Plumbing and Mechanical Codes, Existing Building Codes that focus on renovations and changes of use, and Handicap Building Requirements.

Students, parents or educators not familiar with the trades may be unaware of the many types of trade licenses. For example, in Connecticut, there are currently eight plumbing licenses, based on the scope and nature of work. Licenses include limited or unlimited journeyperson or contractor; sewer, storm and water licenses; and licenses for gasoline, tanks, piping and pumps. Other trades have similar multiple license types.

Certifications are another way to establish credentials. In comparison to licenses, they are usually voluntary and may require a license to take a test. Examples include solar, medical gas, construction management and estimating, and welding. Community colleges, industry groups and associations are common program sources. Safety certifications, such as OSHA 10 or OSHA 30 may be required, particularly for commercial projects.

In the next section we describe six successful tradesmen, in three career stages: Early, Mid and Advanced. "Al's" example on page 13 includes medical gas and well casings certifications and a home improvement registration. Certifications enable you to specialize or expand your services, making you more of a valued employee or respected business owner. In CT, a licensed tradesperson benefits from having a home improvement registration, to cover work outside of his trade. Ex: A plumber replacing a wall disrupted while installing a tub.

College vs. vocational training is not an either/or proposition. Completing night or online classes is entirely possible for a motivated professional, particularly once basic trade requirements are met. Courses in energy conservation, computers, marketing, customer service, and project management can lead to a degree and improve job performance. The natural resources classes Bill took in his B.S. program help him apply science principles on the job. In one class he learned about soil compaction and understands the ability of certain types of soil to support pipes in the ground.

As shown on Bill's profile on page 14, he returned to college full time after serving in combat and working a few years. Between the G.I. Bill and flying helicopters for the CT National Guard he had the financial means to be the "old guy" in the B.S. program. He was 31 when he graduated and worked as a science technician before starting a plumbing & heating apprenticeship with his father-in-law.

<u>Some benefits of college</u>:

College coursework can help you be better on your job and increase career options. Your reading speed and level of comprehension increase; you will sharpen critical thinking habits, improving your problem-solving skills. You build your ability to analyze and evaluate information, and you can present a point of view with a wider vocabulary.   This personal growth is the result of persistent studying on your part – an investment that no one can take away from you.

Specific coursework may put you in line for a promotion to work leader, a role in materials management, or a safety coordinator. Over time, these extra responsibilities usually translate to higher earned wages. As you make career changes, many inspector, teaching and management jobs prefer or require an Associate's or Bachelor's degree. We strongly encourage you to consider adding college credits or a degree to your professional profile; your future self will thank you.

Bill's Top Ten Tips for Success in the Trades

1. ## Develop Discipline
   - **Dress** neatly and appropriately; uniforms are preferred, but if unavailable, use common sense. NEVER wear shorts or T-shirts - they are a safety hazard and look sloppy.
   - **Time** is money; be punctual. Show respect for your company and customers. Leave extra time for traffic and other delays.
   - Swearing is common on work sites, but you can rise above it. Keep your **language and temper** in check. Don't be a hot head.
   - Keep your truck in good condition. A **junk truck** makes people think junk work.

2. ## Be Prepared
   - Keep **safety** glasses, steel-toed shoes, sturdy gloves and other supplies with you; be self-sufficient.
   - Use a metal **clipboard box** to store paper, pens, magnifier, rule and contact information. Don't over-rely on your phone or other devices; sometimes electronics fail us.
   - Purchase the **code books** that govern your trade – tab often-used topics. A list of code publishers is provided in the Resource section. Code-check publications are helpful.

3. ## Pay Attention
   - Construction work is full of **hazards**. Your best defense is staying focused and aware of your surroundings.
   - Keeping your truck and work area **organized** helps you have the right tools and materials to do professional-level work.
   - **Double-check** work orders/specifications to avoid costly errors. Measure twice, cut once.

4. ## Think Big Picture
   - Educate yourself about the **theory** behind the practice. Focusing on the 'doing' vs the 'knowing' limits your ability to identify root causes and solve problems. Read, watch science videos and ask questions.
   - Understand **work project goals** – what does the customer expect?
   - **Who depends on you?** What must go right? How do you fit in?

5. ## Read Instructions & Regulations
   - Unless you've done it 50 times, **review installation guides**.
   - **Check your code book** before forging ahead on a new project.
   - If something seems off, it probably is - **research** it. Avoid a blame game.

6. Stay Humble

- It takes three or four years to become **competent** in a trade, and every year after that requires you learn something new.
- NEVER try to pull something over on **building inspectors** – they have likely seen it before, and it rarely ends well. Don't say "The other Town let me do it this way." Or, "I've done it this way for years." Do not shift the blame by saying "The Building Official told me to do it this way." It is not the Building Official's job to give instructions – only to ensure code compliance. It is the permit holder's responsibility to do the job right. Even inspectors make mistakes, sometimes.
- Guess what? **No one knows everything** (even if they think they do)!

7. Protect Your Reputation

- Maintain a **clean driving record**; no texting or road rage.
- Self-regulate your **social media posts** – they never go away.
- **Alcohol** in moderation; no **drugs** – they affect your judgement. NEVER drink on the job or in route; could result in a lost job or arrest.
- **A criminal record** may keep you from earning a trade license or getting insurance.

8. Become a Life-Long Learner

- **The more you know**, the more valuable you are; the pay will follow.
- Seek out **certifications and specialized classes** – invest in yourself.
- **Plan to go to school for the rest of your life**. Keep up with the times.
- **Don't be a jerk in classes**; listen, take notes, turn off your phone - no side conversations.

9. Join Industry Associations

- You will form **professional friendships** and contacts.
- They help you **stay current** with regulations and trends.
- They offer **resources and training** and identify changes in the field. A list of trade associations is included in the Resources section.

10. Your Boss is Not Your Babysitter

- Keep your **personal problems** largely to yourself.
- **Clean up your area** at the end of each work day.
- Don't worry about **favoritism** – let your work speak for itself.
- **Don't complain** to customers or other contractors about your boss, business or working conditions. If it bothers you so much, get another job.

Meet Six Successful Tradesmen

The following profiles of successful tradesmen are true; other than Bill's, their names and some career details are altered for confidentiality. These are examples of people working in Connecticut, with plumbing, electrical and mechanical (heating and air conditioning) licenses. Two of the tradesmen also acquired licenses or certifications in solar, sheet metal, medical gas, well casings and fire protection.

Training and work experience requirements for other trades such as carpenters, welders, painters, masons, automotive and aviation mechanics will vary, and each State can have different statutory, licensing and certification requirements. Regardless of the specifics, the fundamentals and success factors for building any trade career are similar.

Al's Example: 2nd Generation Business & Industry Leader

Early Career Age 18+	Mid Career Age 30+	Advanced Career Age 50+
• Trade School • Apprentice, Journeyman & Contractor in family plumbing and heating business	• Business Owner • Spokesperson for specialty systems and products • Earned additional licenses in sheet metal and solar • Certifications in well casing and med gas. • Home improvement registration • Continuing Education Classes	• Business Owner • Industry Association Leader • Regulatory Board Chairperson • Real Estate Owner • Plans to pass the business to a son • Continuing Education Classes

Career Highlights:

- Al followed his father in the family business after trade school.
- He established himself as an expert with innovative products.
- Al obtained a variety of related trade licenses and certifications.
- He sponsors employees as apprentices and journeymen.
- Al has a national presence with Industry Associations and chairs a regulatory board at the State level.
- He has vast real estate holdings and one of his sons is in trade school, with plans to lead the 3rd generation business.

Bill's Example: College, Military, Trade Licenses, Building Official & Trainer

Early Career Age 18 +	Mid Career Age 30+	Advanced Career Age 50+
• Public school • A.S. Degree • Military, Active Duty • Manufacturing Job - Manager	• B.S. Degree • National Guard • Apprentice, Journeyman, Contractor • Business Owner • Trade School Instructor	• Plumbing Inspector • Building Official • Continuing Ed Instructor • Association Leader • Trainer, State Job

Career Highlights:

- Bill attended college after public high school; earned an Associates and joined the military as he faced being drafted. He served in combat.
- Upon discharge he worked for three years in a manufacturing company,
- He then returned to college under the G.I. Bill, earned a bachelor's degree and joined the National Guard, as a part-time job during college.
- After graduation he worked in a science job for a year, before starting plumbing & heating apprenticeships with his father-in-law
- After seven years he bought the family business, with a contractor license.
- He began teaching trade school at night.
- At age 50 he sold the family business and became a Plumbing Inspector for a municipality; he earned his Assistant Building Official and Building Official licenses. He became active in Industry Associations, including leadership.
- He developed courses and taught continuing education on the weekends to journeymen and contractors, due to new State licensing requirements.
- Bill retired at 67 and worked part time as a Special Inspector and Assistant Building Inspector.
- At 73, he teaches State classes full-time for people preparing for B.O. exams

Curt's Example: Life-long Electrician & Inspector

Early Career Age 18+	Mid Career Age 30+	Advanced Career Age 50+
• Trade School • Electrical Journeyman, Apprentice • Journeyman at several small businesses	• Contractor/Foreman for medium sized and large businesses • Heavy commercial and residential work • Business Owner • Continuing Education Classes	• Electrical Inspector for a municipality • Assistant Building Official License • Continuing Education Classes

Career Highlights:

- Curt has worked in the electrical trade field since Trade school graduation.
- He worked for several electrical contractors in both residential and commercial areas, including healthcare, education and State projects.
- Curt operated his own business for 10 years before working as an Electrical Inspector in a municipality.
- He joined Industry Associations and completes continuing education requirements.
- Curt served for many years as the electrician for a large fair in his hometown.
- A sample resume based on Curt's experience is shown on page 28.

Tom's Example: Electrical Installation Jobs and Non-Profit Leader

Early Career Age 18+	Mid Career Age 30+	Advanced Career Age 50+
• Trade School • Security alarm installer • Low voltage license	• Installer for residential & commercial • Started and led a community non-profit that offers youth programs	• Installer for residential & commerical • Non-profit now offers jobs and life skill programs for a tri-town area

Career Highlights:

- Tom started installing security alarms after completing Trade School, earning a low-voltage license.
- He presently has a telecommunications installation job that involves splicing, cable repair and replacement, and pole repair/ replacement. He now has 32 years of experience.
- Tom's leadership of a community non-profit includes training and internships in the trades for people ages 17-24. He oversees 8 part-time employees and secures funding through grants and positive outcomes. He has led the non-profit for 22 years, while working full-time. Tom is celebrated as a change agent within his community.

Pete's Example: Trade School, Plumber, Military, College, Engineer

Early Career Age 18+	Mid Career Age 30+	Advanced Career Age 50+
• Trade School • Apprentice, Journeyman, Contractor • Plumbing Jobs • Active Military • College - A.S.	• Engineering job for a global company • Continued college at night - B.S. • Earned patents for mechanical design. • Continuing Education Classes	• Design & production Engineering Director • Continuing Education Classes

Career Highlights:

- After trade school Pete worked as a plumbing apprentice and journeyman and went on to obtain his contractor license. He also earned heating and fire protection licenses.
- With 3 years' work experience he joined the Air Force full time, where he trained and worked as a mechanic on jet engines.
- Upon military discharge Pete went to college full time, using the G.I. Bill.
- He earned an Associate's degree and started work in the engineering field.
- Pete earned his bachelor's degree after ten years of night school, taking a break when he assumed a higher-level job.
- He is currently in management with a global company and has numerous registered patents in tool design.
- Pete maintains his contractor license active and fulfills his continuing education requirements.
- He keeps his trades skills current through home improvement projects.

Henry's Example: Heating/Plumbing & School Maintenance Jobs

Early Career Age 18+	Mid Career Age 30+	Advanced Career Age 50+
• Public High School • Trade School at night in heating • Oil Burner License and Job • Trade School at night in plumbing	• Apprentice and Journeyman in a plumbing & heating business • Continuing Education Classes	• Plumber within a public school maintenance department • Continuing Education Classes

Career Highlights:

- Henry graduated from high school and took night classes to earn an oil burner license.
- He worked for a medium-sized heating company and continued taking night classes to earn his plumbing license.
- His next job was with a small plumbing and heating business, largely doing residential work.
- Henry completed his required continuing education classes along the way.
- His advanced career is working within the public education system, as a plumbing tradesperson in the maintenance department.
- He continues to complete all continuing education requirements to maintain his licenses.

Mid and Advanced Career Changes

"It does not matter how slowly you go as long as you do not stop." — Confucius

As shown in the six examples of successful tradesmen, career development can involve large or small steps:

- Gaining additional trade licenses and certifications
- Building mechanical skills in military service
- Working as a manufacturing Customer Service Manager
- Getting a college degree, in addition to trade licenses
- Managing an independent contracting business
- Teaching night school and continuing education classes
- Taking a leadership role within an industry association
- Gaining commercial and residential trade experience
- Acting as a Foreman on medium to large projects
- Representing specialty systems and products
- Getting Inspector or Building Official licenses

Some of these tradesmen took several of the above steps during a 30 to 40-year career. Even jobs that are outside of a typical trade program build skills that add up to success: Doing novel and challenging work increases your brain's learning and memory capacity. Or, as Helen Hayes famously put it: "If you rest, you rust." Successful people continually push themselves outside of their comfort zones; typically, adults don't like to be novices.

Job or career changes require giving up what is familiar, taking on new duties, and proving yourself all over again. Often the full set of responsibilities and job conditions are not initially apparent, which can cause a 'longing for the past', even if it was far from perfect. At least you knew the rules!

For example, working in a school system may subject you to a lack of appreciation for your credentials and responsibilities. Public school teachers may still be in the "college is best" bubble and think your job is not professional. Or managers in a municipality may not understand or respect building codes, and pressure an Inspector or Building Official to approve faulty work by a politically connected contractor.

When Georgian taught continuing education business classes to plumbing contractors, it was common to hear that "If I knew about these strict labor laws, I would not have started my own business." Gaining a clear-eyed view of the pros and cons of a major change requires:

1. <u>Knowing your work preferences and strengths</u>. If you value security over risk taking, starting your own business will be especially stressful. If you are calling the shots as a Foreman, working in a bureaucratic organization will require a great deal of restraint. If you thrive on solving challenging technical problems, becoming a teacher may not be satisfying. Office and teaching jobs involve working with software programs – is that something you learn quickly? Career preferences can change over time; finances, the business climate, working long hours and physical issues can affect what matters most and what you are willing to give up.

2. <u>Looking before you leap</u>. Take the time to talk to as many people as possible who have direct experience in the area you are considering. This is especially important for starting your own business. While you don't want to be bombarded by negativity, you need to assess how you will get the required financial, legal, marketing, risk management and technology support. Taking a class in business management, through a trade association, adult education class or community college would be a wise investment. If you are interviewed for a project management job with a new company, ask about expected levels of travel and overtime. If the economy declines, is the job subject to layoff? Will you be given a company vehicle, or are you looking at putting a lot of miles on your own truck?

3. <u>Assessing where this change fits in your overall career</u>. If it doesn't work out, will it be easy to go back to what you've been doing -- or would you look for something else? Is this opportunity something you've always wanted to do, and you have a Plan B? Does the job offer security, such as a hope of earning a pension – and you are prepared to stick it out, no matter what? Age, physical capacity and financial obligations are common decision factors. One benefit of being in the trades is that if you keep your licenses current, there is usually a way to get work, using your toolbox. Bill stresses that once you earn a license, never let it lapse.

Making job or career changes requires a healthy dose of realistic optimism and the ability to face fear. You may underestimate that your skills are transferable – often the biggest obstacle is self-doubt. Support comes in many forms; the key is to seek it out. You create career options by trying new things, continually learning and forming relationships within your community and industry. Stay open to future possibilities.

Resume and Interview Tips

One important key to success is self-confidence. An important key to self-confidence is preparation. Arthur Ashe

Employers are usually pressed for time: Your resume should be a snapshot. While there is no gold standard for a resume; strive for the following:

- Use white space, bold font and underlining to highlight key facts.
- No gaps in time – account for any employment interruption – such as attending a school or military duty.
- Provide names and locations of employers; street addresses not required.
- Use short phrases about key responsibilities – full sentences not required.
- List educational degrees, certifications, classes – show you are a learner.
- Show involvement in community / volunteer activities and awards.
- List membership in industry organizations – leadership roles a plus.
- <u>No</u> personal information - marital status, children, religion, date of birth.

Two sample resumes, using the same general format, are on pages 28 and 29. Details about employers are deleted for confidentiality, and Bill's resume is condensed to fit on one page. Two pages are acceptable if you need to elaborate on a past job for a specific application. Municipal jobs may have statutory requirements and therefore do not need descriptions, unless you are changing states.

A common resume mistake is to create a highly detailed task list. If, for example, you learned vehicle maintenance skills while serving in the National Guard, you do not need to provide the model numbers of vehicles you fixed. Focus on the type of experience you gained, such as working with heavy equipment or driving a vehicle requiring a CDL. If someone wants to know more, they can ask you during the interview. You can bring back up information to an interview.

Resume and Interview Tips (cont'd)

Don't overstate your experience or make things up. It is easy for an employer to get information on you, and that would question your integrity.

Be prepared to explain why you left school, or an employer. Be honest and thoughtful.

#7 on Bill's Top Ten Tips is "Protect Your Reputation." Job hunting should include a review of your social media sites – what image are you projecting?

Large organizations may use screening software. Your resume should include key words from the job posting, such as a CDL license, a certification or supervisory experience.

How to prepare for an interview:

- Look up information about the company or Town you are interviewing with. This will help you answer a question of "Why do you want to work for us?"
- Practice your success stories and answers to common questions. Examples are provided on the following pages. Some interviewers lack experience asking questions or may only focus on the technical requirements of the job. Try to be prepared for a wide range of questions: You may be asked to respond to a hypothetical situation.
- Bring a notebook and a few copies of your resume to the interview; in a panel interview, not everyone may have your resume.
- Jot down questions or important points you want to make in the interview; view the conversation as two-way, not an inquisition.
- Wear neat clothes & clean shoes. You are not on a job site; dress up.
- Tell people in advance if you are using them as a reference.
- Do a practice drive to the interview site and leave time for rush hour traffic.

Things to remember during an interview:

- **Body language** is important. Do not cross your arms, lean back or tap on a table. Use a firm handshake, good eye contact and polite language.
- **Be comfortable with silence**. Take a moment to collect your thoughts when asked a question, and do not ramble on if the interviewer pauses.
- **Go with the flow.** If you are in a formal interview process, do not show impatience if it appears no one has looked at your resume.
- **Do not apologize** for any lack of formal education or specific experience. Be proud of your accomplishments and show you are always willing to learn.
- Contrary to conventional advice, **it is wise to admit to a weakness**. Keep it job-specific: *I know I will need to step up my computer skills in this job*.
- No matter how well deserved, **do not make insulting remarks about your last employer.** It ends up putting you, not them, in a bad light.
- **It is acceptable to ask** for an approximate time when the hiring decision will be made, or if the interviewer needs any additional information.
- **Send a thank you note or email** after the interview, even if you are not sure you will accept the job. It shows respect for the interviewer's time.

Sample Interview Questions

- Warm-up: How was your commute in this weather /traffic?
- How did you hear about this position?
- Tell us about yourself.
- How did you get into this field?
- What are your professional goals?
- Why are you interested in working for this Company/Town/School?
- Why are looking to leave your current position?
- What motivated you to join, and leave, your previous jobs?
- Describe what you do in your current job. What do you like most? Least?

- Can you give me two strengths and two areas you could improve?
- Does this salary in this job meet your requirements?
- On a scale of 1 to 5 (5 being highest) – rate your ability to perform each of these core job responsibilities…. Including technology.
- What technical resources would you rely on in this job?
- What are your biggest accomplishments in doing this type of work?
- How would you describe your attendance and ability to meet deadlines?
- Please explain the gap in employment between _____ and _____.
- What things have you done on your own, to prepare for your next job?
- Tell us about a time you knew were right, but still had to follow rules.
- Tell us about a time your workday ended before you could meet all your deadlines. Or a project was under-resourced.
- Faced with competing demands, how do you determine your priorities?
- Describe a time when you successfully accomplished a difficult goal.
- Describe a time when something went wrong at work, and your response.
- What would former co-workers or supervisors say about you?
- Give us an example of a conflict with a co-worker. What happened?
- Describe any ethical dilemma you faced at work, and what you did.
- Tell us about a time you changed your style to work better with a person.
- Describe a time you had to plan with incomplete information.

For Management Positions:

- Tell us about some of your achievements as a Manager or Supervisor.
- Do you have hire/fire experiences? If so, what happened when you made a poor hire – when someone did not work out?
- Describe your experiences in using data to make decisions and prepare reports.
- How have your resolved conflict within a group? With someone you reported to?
- How would you go about establishing credibility with a new team?
- What software programs are you familiar with?

- Describe your management style.
- Do you consider yourself to have good people skills?
- How would you handle pressure from a person with political leverage?
- Rate your writing and communication skills.
- Do you have experience with developing budgets, policies & instructions?

Common Interview Concerns:

Regarding weaknesses – identify something that is real but is not a deal breaker – such as speaking at a Council meeting, preparing reports and budgets using a municipal software program, doing performance appraisals on staff, developing a specialized training program. Offer how you are taking steps to work on the weakness, through reading, internet videos, taking classes, etc. Then move on.

Regarding your background – work experience and education. Yes, focus on the job requirements (Knowledge, Skills, Abilities) but it is often relevant to include military and volunteer activities, which may have honed skills in map reading, coaching others, working in a team, mechanical repair, school budgets, organizational efficiencies, etc.

Tricky technical questions – avoid getting flustered if asked about a code or regulation without the benefit of reference materials. As Bill stated in his "Top Ten Tips for Success in the Trades", don't guess. Describe what steps you would take to find the answer to the question, such as checking a specific section of a code book or relevant document.

Highly suggested approach: Think back on your experiences and develop 3 or 4 "success stories" that illustrate your strengths. These may be in the areas of:

- Strong work ethic
- problem solving
- conflict resolution
- implementing safety measures
- influencing key people to move forward on a project
- coming up with novel or creative ways to work around an obstacle
- demonstrating leadership – resisting taking an easy way out
- maintaining ethical standards in a stressful situation

Success stories are listed in Georgian's "Top Ten Tips for Career Success." They also relate to the third factor identified as making a big difference in your career options: Self-awareness regarding personal strengths.

<u>Think of creating your success stories in three parts:</u>

(1) What happened?
(2) Why did you do it?
(3) How did this help the company?

Here are three samples:

<u>Strength: Dependability</u>

In three years, I have only taken four days off for illness or a family emergency. I know my boss is counting on me, and companies lose money when people don't show up.

<u>Strength: Initiative</u>

Once I volunteered to accept a materials delivery on a job site on a Sunday morning, which was essential for meeting a deadline. This project was important to the company.

<u>Strength: Customer Service Skills</u>

In working with an unhappy customer, I asked a series of questions to identify points of confusion about a warranty on a hot water heater. I saved the account by not minimizing her concerns and referred her to my boss, who quickly followed up.

<u>Keep your success stories short, practice them, and use them to provide examples.</u>

SAMPLE RESUME – EXPERIENCED ELECTRICIAN

Name, Phone, Email

EXPERIENCE

2015 - Present	<u>Assistant Building Official</u>, *Town/City,* CT	*Jobs are defined in State Statues; no description needed*
2007 – 2015	<u>Electrical Inspector</u>, *Town/City,* CT	

1999 - Present   <u>Electrical Contractor</u>, Self-Employed – *Insert Company Name*
Fulfills trade contracts for industrial, commercial and residential projects, across Connecticut, including estimating, purchasing, billing.

1985 - 1999   <u>Apprentice, Journeyman, Contractor and Foreman On-Site.</u> Worked for two electrical companies, with increasing levels of responsibility. Projects included new and existing residential installations, new construction of healthcare facilities, existing educational building upgrades, life safety systems installations, exterior site and sports complex lighting and power.

<u>Specific projects</u>: Manufacturing plant relocation; large-scale healthcare facilities, new and existing construction; State office building upgrades and college campus upgrades. (*Insert organizational project names / locations*)

TRADE LICENSES   State of CT: <u>Building Official</u> and <u>Electrical Inspector</u>
<u>Electrical Contractor</u>, E1

EDUCATION   Continuing education classes as required by the State of CT. for maintaining Electrical and Building Official licenses.

State of CT Office of Education and Data Management: Pre-licensure programs - 2007, 2009, 2011.

High School Graduate

TRADE MEMBERSHIPS   International Association of Electrical Inspectors (IAEI); National Fire Protection Association (NFPA)

COMMUNITY CONTRIBUTIONS   Electrician of Record for a Town's 'Extravaganza' event for 20 years. Member / Volunteer; Little League and Field Building Committee.

EXPERIENCE

2017 – Present	Trainer, State of CT Pre-Licensure Program (Full Time)
2014 – 2017	Part-time Assistant Building Official and Special Inspector
2007 – 2014	Building Official, City in Connecticut. (Retired)
1995 - 2007	Plumbing & Mechanical Inspector, City in CT.

Jobs are defined by State Statue

2005 - 2017	Instructor, Center for Occupational Development & Education. Developed / delivered continuing education Plumbing classes.
2005 - 2008	Instructor, Plumbing Apprenticeship Program, Wilcox Technical School, CT.
1986 - 1988	
1989 - 1996	Owner, Farkas Plumbing & Heating, CT. Residential, commercial and service: Repair, remodeling, new construction.
1979 - 1989	Apprentice, Journeyman, Contractor: Farkas Plumbing & Heating, One year as Service Rep; Standard Plumbing Supply, CT.
1977 - 1979	Research Technician, Agricultural Experiment Station, State of CT.
1971 - 1975	Manager, Customer Service and Lab Technician. The Napier Co.

EDUCATION

1975 - 1977	B.S., Natural Resource Conservation, University of Connecticut
1965 - 1968	A.S., Liberal Arts, Northwestern Michigan Community College

CERTIFICATIONS & LICENSES: CT Building Official; Plumbing Inspector; Plumbing, P1; Heating S3; Fire Protection, F1; Sheet Metal SM-1, Oil Burner cert; Solar, ST-1

MILITARY

1975 - 1978	Chief Warrant Officer, CW3 - Helicopter Pilot. Army National Guard.
1968 - 1971	Chief Warrant Officer, CW2 - Helicopter Pilot. U.S. Army - Vietnam

MEMBERSHIPS: *Past Board President*, Center for Occupational Development and Education (C.O.D.E.). *Past President and Secretary,* CT Association of Plumbing & Heating Inspectors; CT Building Officials Association; Rod & Gun Club.

APPRECIATION: CT Plumbing, Heating & Cooling Contractors; 2007, 2012
Technical Trade Association Committee, 2006
Library of Congress, Veteran's History Project: *You Tube* Interview, 2013

Career Development: Georgian's Top Ten Tips for Trade Success

1. <u>Update Your Resume</u>
   - **Twice a year, review your resume** and add new accomplishments. Don't wait until a crisis requires you to look for a new job.
   - Resume drafts usually have too much detail. **Keep some material for the job interview**. Refer to the sample resumes on the previous pages.
   - **Use your resume review as motivation** for increasing your skills and certifications. If nothing has changed in a year, time to seek new credentials!

2. <u>Know Your Success Stories</u>
   - **Everyone likes a good story**, including people who can help you advance. Reflect on times when you applied your skills to a challenging work situation.
   - In telling your story, **keep it short and focus on how your efforts produced a desirable outcome.** Did you solve a stubborn problem? Calm down a customer? Teach a skill?
   - Without bragging, **highlight your unique mix of skills, abilities and personal traits** in telling your story. Helpful for a job interview or when seeking new responsibilities.

3. <u>Plan to Shift from Physical Work</u>
   - As shown in the six examples of successful tradesmen, **it is common to seek work with fewer physical demands as you age.**
   - **Supervising others, working as an inspector or teaching trade classes** are examples of applying trade skills in mid or advanced career stages.
   - **Prepare for the long haul by expanding your mind as well as your hands-on skills**. Be willing to look like a novice in order to learn something new.

4. <u>Exercise Your Brain</u>
   - If you truly want a successful trade career, **be curious and seek out new experiences**. Challenge some of your own assumptions and consider other points of view.
   - Charles Schultz, the Peanuts cartoonist, said "Life is like a 10-speed bicycle. Most of us have gears we never use." While solid habits can help you be productive, **becoming complacent is deadly for careers.** Opportunities will pass you by.
   - **Practice ways to improve your memory**: Actively listen and avoid multi-tasking. Sound sleep is essential to transfer short term to long term memory.
   - Exercise and socializing also are linked to **good brain health** over time.

5. Know Your Learning Style

- There are at least 7 learning styles / forms of intelligence – **most people in the trades think in terms of physical space and learn by figuring things out by hand**.
- **Tailor your study skills to your learning style**. Ex: Walk around while reciting something you need to memorize; take 5-minute breaks every 20-30 minutes.
- **Develop a habit of thinking critically**: Evaluate information using observation, experience, reflection and sound reasoning. Seek clarity and accuracy.

6. Choose the Company You Keep

- **The people you spend the most time with** influence your levels of confidence and self-control. Strong-willed friends can help you avoid unwise risks when stressed.
- **Stay connected to people with good problem-solving skills, goals and discipline**.
- Loyalty is a virtue but **limit your time with old friends that have bad habits.**

7. Get a Little Better Every Day

- Scott Adams, the Dilbert cartoonist, believes that **stacking one modest skill on top of another one** can create something special. Example: Making a presentation at a Trade School builds speaking skills.
- **Make a new routine** by piggybacking one small behavior onto an existing one. Ex: Charge your phone, put your keys near the door, then lay out a clean shirt.
- **Success begets success.** Develop discipline and you will seek more challenges.

8. Seek Mentors & Role Models

- **Observe people who have made successful career shifts** in the trades and think about how you can develop options for yourself.
- **Volunteer to help a more experienced person do a good deed,** such as building a ramp for a veteran. Extend yourself, and others become inclined to help you.
- **Seek advice.** Honor the person's time; prepare questions for the conversation.

9. Share Your Talents

- **Spend time with someone just starting out**. Be interested, no judgement.
- **Be generous when asked for help** but watch out for working without insurance.
- **Have fun** by working at a community event; remember why you like your work.

10. Follow Bill's Top Ten Tips for Success in the Trades (pages 10 & 11)

"Retirement" Jobs – A Victory Lap!

Working past retirement age has the same intrinsic benefits as earlier in life: Your brain stays nimble, you maintain relationships with colleagues, and you are acknowledged for your expertise and contributions. Getting paid can be icing on the cake or can fill a real financial need. Of course, every job has drawbacks.

For example, Bill worked as a Special Inspector Technician for an engineering firm right after he retired at 67. He stayed 18 months, learning a lot about the requirements of mixing and pouring concrete on commercial jobs, as well as inspecting soils and wood. However, standing in wet pits and trying to stop a concrete delivery that did not meet specifications were hassles that outweighed the benefits of the job. While the company espoused safety, he was expected to answer his phone while driving – which gave him a second traffic violation in 50 years. But the job did provide a bridge to other opportunities.

Bill then filled in as an Assistant Building Official for a small Town, mostly working to close open permits for roofs and pools. He also developed and delivered continuing education classes at this time. Three years after retiring he was selected for his current job as a Trainer for the State of Connecticut. Georgian sees this as a victory lap for him – he puts the building course material in the context of his forty years of trade experience – including his Special Inspection job!

Organizations and colleges are taking a lead in advocating work after retirement. AARP sponsored a seminar called "Your Next Act in Manufacturing" with the public schools in our town, inviting trade retirees to consider becoming mentors to teachers of carpentry, drafting, and computer-aided design. Teaching at a community college was also a possible opportunity for the retirees. A Connecticut State University, which is certified as "Age-Friendly" also supported this seminar, in terms of learning how to transfer hands-on experience to the classroom.

In an AARP magazine the author David Saperstein, whose book inspired the movie "Cocoon", explored how work can contribute to aging well, and how he does not see retirement as an ending. (AARP Bulletin/Real Possibilities - January February 2019) The authors, who are both working after retirement age, encourage you to think about sharing your lifetime of expertise through teaching, mentoring or perhaps working at the counter of a supply house. The younger generations need you!

Resources

Codes & Standards publications used in Connecticut: States may vary.

- **NFPA – National Fire Protection Association**
- **NFPA 70 – Electrical Code**
- **NFPA 54 – Gas Code**
- **NFPA 58 – Propane Code**
- **NFPA 31 – Oil burner & Oil Equipment Code**

International Code Council: iccsafe.org
Members include state, county and municipal code enforcement and fire officials, architects, engineers, builders, contractors, elected officials and manufacturers.

Code Check   codecheck.com
Key to the Codes: The Most Widely Used Building Code Reference Series in the U.S.; Building, Electrical, Plumbing and Mechanical Codes

Trade-Related State Agencies & Departments in Connecticut – States will vary

Department of Consumer Protection –Trade licenses, business practices and more.
Department of Administrative Services – Licensing, Certifications & Building Codes
Department of Revenue Services – Business sales tax and payments
Department of Labor – Protects & promotes the interests of Connecticut workers
Connecticut Technical Education and Career System

Trade Associations, programs and publications … Just to name a few

Plumbing-Heating-Cooling Contractors Association - phccweb.org
PHCC provides legislative advocacy, education and training to approximately 3,300 plumbing and HVAC open shop and union businesses and 65,000 technicians.

Independent Electrical Contractors – ieci.org
IEC represents over 3,000-member businesses throughout the U.S. and educates over 12,000 electricians and systems professionals each year through world-class training programs.

American Welding Society   aws.org

American Welding Society aws.org

The Academy for Professional Painters paintersacademy.com

Painting and Decorating Contractors of America pdca.org
PDCA offers 310,000 contractor members opportunities to develop through participation in education programs, local networking meetings, & use of PDCA Industry Standards.

ABC: Associated Builders & Contractors, Inc. **AGC**: Associated General Contractors of America **AIC**: American Institute of Constructors

Solar Energy Industries Association seia.org

Contractor magazine contractormag.com

Harbor Freight Tools for Schools - harborfreighttoolsforschools.org
This program was started by its CEO and Founder, Eric Smidt, with deep respect for the intelligence and creativity of people who work with their hands. It includes teaching excellence awards and a "Let's Build It" initiative of nationally recognized industry educators.

SkillsUSA: Champions at Work   www.skillsusa.org
SkillsUSA is a partnership of students, teachers & industry, working together to ensure America has a skilled workforce.

Mike Rowe Foundation – mikeroweworks.com
In 2008, Mike created the mikeroweWORKS Foundation to launch a national PR campaign for skilled labor … and it now offers scholarships and job postings.

You Tube videos mention in this Handbook - Search by the title:

Interview with William J. Lussier, Vietnam War Veteran. CCSU Veterans History Project

Melissa Sheffy & Georgian Lussier – Construction Careers! (WPAA-TV)

Videos mentioned in this Handbook:

PBS "Masters of the Building Arts" - pbs.org/show/good-work

History Channel "Modern Marvels" series – history.com/shows/modern-marvel
Titles include: Renewable Energy, Pumps, Hydraulics, Water, Gasoline, Oil, Gas Tech, etc.

Author's Biographies

<u>Bill Lussier</u>

Bill's background and experiences are well documented in this Handbook, including serving as an example of a successful tradesperson (page 14) and his resume (page 29).

As he is working full-time, Bill does not closely monitor his email during working hours. Please contact <u>georgian@successintheskilledtrades.com</u> and visit us on Facebook – "Building Success in the Trades."

Here is a fun fact about Bill. In 2016 he designed and built a wood-burning pizza oven in the backyard. It takes three to four hours to reach 600+ degrees, and less than five minutes to cook a pizza. Of course, he followed safety precautions! Not to brag, but Bill's results are as good as the famous New Haven pizzas.

Authors' Biographies

Georgian Lussier

Georgian is the daughter of a plumber. Her Dad, George Farkas, became a plumbing and heating tradesman in the '50s. The son of Hungarian immigrants, he joined the Navy to fight in WW II and served as a hydraulics mechanic on a PBY. Starting as a roofer, George ultimately became a Superintendent for a large commercial company before being downsized and starting his own business, which Bill later joined. He was active in his local Plumbing, Heating and Cooling Contractor's Association and was named as a Contractor of the Year.

For over 5 years Georgian developed and taught business classes through Connecticut's continuing education requirements for licensed plumbing contractors. In 2006 she wrote five articles for Contractor magazine.

Georgian's career in Human Resources spans 40 years; she held technical and leadership jobs in large insurance companies before starting her own consulting practice in 1994.

She has served many industries and has specialties in pay systems, training and organizational development. Georgian also provides resume writing and career counseling to individuals, including those in the trades. For seven years she hosted and produced a community TV show for women and has served on several boards of directors. She authored several publications for women and wrote two e-books on developing talent through Get To The Point Books.

Georgian has a B.S. in English and a M.S. in Organizational Behavior. Visit our website, successintheskilledtrades.com and our Facebook page, "Building Success in the Trades."

*****

Bill and Georgian have been married over 40 years and are pleased their daughter inherited Bill's mechanical aptitude! This Handbook celebrates the talents of colleagues in the trades with hope that it inspires others to rethink a trade career.

This Handbook is available on Amazon.com.